A Man's
Guide
to the
Justification
of
Golf

A MAN'S GUIDE TO THE

JUSTIFICATION OF

Golf

Bob Peck
and
Sandy Silver

ANDREWS AND McMEEL
A Universal Press Syndicate Company
Kansas City

ISBN: 0-8362-2755-7

Library of Congress Catalog Card Number: 96-86679

INTRODUCTION

Rationalization is the lowest form of human thinking. Unfortunately, the dedicated golfer must sometimes resort to it in order to keep from losing his mind . . . or what is left of it.

Faced with a myriad of obstacles that threaten to prevent his enjoyment of the greatest of all pastimes, the golfer requires a means by which to free himself from the shackles of home and office.

The following is guaranteed to provide the dedicated golfer with a choice of reasons to justify why he needs to play golf and leave his guilt behind.

I Must Play Golf Today:

MEDICAL REASONS

► My heart rate goes up when I hit a good shot.

► My heart rate really goes up when I hit a bad shot.

► Getting in and out of a cart is low-impact exercise.

► My five iron is low-impact exercise.

► The fluorescent light in my office is un-healthy.

► Sunshine increases my libido.

► There are no fat
grams in eating
your words.

► Golf is a combined, whole-body workout.

▶ *Lean* and *hard* can describe your stomach, driver, or score.

► Learning holistic golf includes two-putting.

► Genetically, I am predisposed to play golf because my father played golf.

► Playing in the dark prevents night blindness.

► "Use it or lose it" not only applies to muscle conditioning but also to my golf game.

► Sweat removes toxins.

► The result of drinking a lot of beer also removes toxins.

► Pulling your ball
out of the cup is like
touching your toes.

► Climbing in and out
of the golf cart is like
doing step aerobics.

I Must Play Golf Today:

MONETARY REASONS

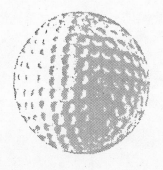

► The guys I play with
always lose.

► There is a five-dollar limit (lie).

► I will spend all my winnings on my wife (lie).

➤ I have won the last ten times we have played.

➤ Two of the guys I bet with have bad backs . . . and bad games.

• • • • • • • • • • • • • • • •

► It is my job—some-
times I even get paid.

► I will find at least forty
balls . . . big savings.

• • • • • • • • • • • • • • • •

► There may be gold instead of sand in the next bunker.

► My score reversed is this week's winning lotto number.

• • • • • • • • • • • • • • • •

► I never give back the coin when someone else marks my ball.

• • • • • • • • • • • • • •

I Must Play Golf Today:

SELF-IMPROVEMENT
REASONS

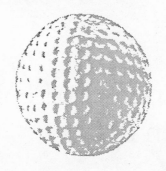

► My inner child plays well.

► My outer child plays even better.

► My biorhythms need tuning.

► I need to bond with my driver.

► My self-esteem improves with a good putt.

► I will grow rich by visualizing that I will receive money on the nineteenth hole.

• • • • • • • • • • • • • • • •

► To be completely
centered, I must
play golf.

• • • • • • • • • • • • • • •

► I must meditate be-
fore I play golf—not
during my swing.

► My mantra is "make
the putt . . . make the
putt . . ."

► My idea of harmonic convergence is when my driver collides with the ball and makes that sweet sound.

► I practice yoga while waiting for the group ahead of me to hit.

I Must Play Golf Today:

BUSINESS REASONS

► The boss made
me do it.

► Scoping prospects.

► The *Wall Street Journal* is sold at the course.

► Caddies are great networkers.

► Customer satisfaction includes playing golf with my customer and saying "great shot" a lot.

► Golf is a win/win
situation for me
and the client . . .
especially if the
client wins.

► I can dictate a memo
from the pay phone
at the turn.

➤ "Put first things first"
. . . therefore, I must
play golf first thing.

➤ I must check out the calling radius of my cellular phone and pager.

➤ Laptop computers work in golf carts.

· · · · · · · · · · · · · · · ·

► Playing golf for four
hours with a client is
better than drinking
for four hours with a
client.

► "Taking Care of
Business" is a good
song on the golf
course.

➤ I need to spend up to my expense-account limit.

► Ready golf is a proactive answer to slow play.

I Must Play Golf Today:

WEATHER REASONS

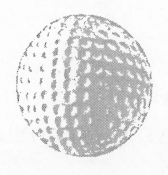

► Sunburn clears up
my skin.

► Cloudy days cut
down on harmful
glare.

► Over ten degrees is okay; anything below that is just too cold.

► Rain is okay . . .
forgot my deodorant
anyway.

► Snow is invigorating.

► Ice is only a problem on the cart path.

► Winter rules are a real thing.

► The "casual water" rule was written for floods.

• • • • • • • • • • • • • • • •

► I really look good in
sweaters.

• • • • • • • • • • • • • • • •

➤ It is hard to over-swing in thermal underwear.

► I have been looking
for an excuse to use
that new umbrella.

► Tornadoes are not
a problem because
there are no mobile
homes near the golf
course.

► Getting hit by light-
ning saves money
on cremation.

► Hurricanes are only a
problem on holes
into the wind.

I Must Play Golf Today:

HOLIDAY REASONS

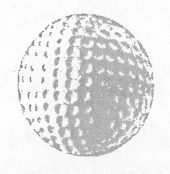

► Turkeys take at least four hours to bake.

► My mother-in-law suggested I play thirty-six holes.

➤ It is a Christmas gift
to myself . . . yeah,
right.

➤ I must wear my new
Christmas outfit.

➤ You can never play
with your wife in a
Valentine's Day
scramble . . . it is
a rule, hon.

► Saint Patrick's Day is a national golf holiday since golf was invented in Ireland. (Scotland is close to Ireland!)

► Thanksgiving is the day we concede all four-foot putts.

► Labor Day is
designed as a
golf holiday.

► The Fourth of July is actually "Golf Patriots Day," and I must play to be a good American.

► I must play on New Year's Day because I am in a hurry to establish a handicap.

► You hunt Easter eggs your way . . . I'll hunt them my way.

► Twenty-seven holes
are a must on the
vernal equinox.

➤ Playing on Memorial
Day . . . a fitting trib-
ute to our war dead.

I Must Play Golf Today:

ROMANTIC REASONS

▶ Golf raises my testosterone level.

▶ The blowing wind also raises my testosterone level.

► I will buy you any-
thing your heart
desires with the
money I win.

► Relationships are strengthened by playing golf.

► "Spanking the puppy"
is not limited to golf.

► I learned the meaning of commitment from playing golf . . . right.

➤ "Two days of week-
end golf equals two
romantic dinners with
you, dear."

► I will be home by seven to take that *Cosmo* quiz with you.

• • • • • • • • • • • • • • • • •

➤ The wife looks much more attractive after a tough day on the links.

• • • • • • • • • • • • • • • •

► In between shots, I think about you, dear.

► Golf teaches the patience required for successful foreplay.

I Must Play Golf Today:

ENVIRONMENTAL
REASONS

➤ The golf birdie is an endangered species.

➤ The golf balls from the male golf birdie are all endangered for other reasons.

► Recycling golf balls
is politically correct.

► Replacing divots is not only politically correct, it will allow you to receive praise and respect from others, leading to increased popularity.

► "Nature's way" is not only a laxative but also a good roll by the ball on the green.

► Someone needs to play in the dark to test fluorescent-colored balls.

► It is my early-morning
job to see if golf balls
have any harmful
effects on greens
with fresh morning
dew on them.

► I must search for lost
balls with hope of
finding beer cans
to recycle.

► I must occasionally
check water quality
by hitting and retriev-
ing golf balls in water
hazards.

► The spikes in my golf shoes help aerate the course.

► Fart gas helps replenish the ozone.

► I will donate my
winnings to
Greenpeace.

► Dimples on golf balls help trap harmful polycarbons.

► My ball retriever doubles as a water purification device.

I Must Play Golf Today:

RELIGIOUS REASONS

► I speak about God
on almost every shot.

► Sometimes the clouds take the shape of the Virgin Mary (she also works in the snack bar).

► Sundays are made for golf.

► Replacing divots is necessary to get into golf heaven.

► Hitting a perfect drive is a religious experience.

➤ "Laughter is good for the soul"—plenty of that on a golf course.

► I must practice
wisdom (knowing
when not to bet).

► I must practice virtue
(knowing when not
to brag).

► I will pray over all ten-foot putts.

► Making an eagle feels close to divine inspiration.

I Must Play Golf Today:

UNSELFISH REASONS

► Wives and girlfriends need time for themselves.

● ● ● ● ● ● ● ● ● ● ● ● ● ● ● ●

► The foursome needs to be exposed to my wonderful personality.

● ● ● ● ● ● ● ● ● ● ● ● ● ● ● ●

► Holes in one need witnesses.

► People need golf advice from me.

► Greenskeepers need
"attaboys."

► Pro shops need
increased sales.

► Lost balls must be found . . . someone has to do it.

I Must Play Golf Today:

PHILOSOPHICAL
REASON

➤ If a tree falls on the golf course, I need to be there to hear it.

I Must Play Golf Today:

SCIENTIFIC REASONS

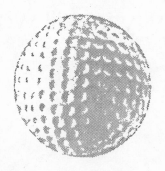

▸ Sinking a putt is
a way to test that
gravity is still working.

► My golf partner's
arthritis is an
excellent predictor
of changes in
barometric pressure.

► I promise not to smash any atoms when I pound my club on the ground in disgust.

► What some people call throwing a club is actually a demonstration of aerodynamic principles.

► The theory that hot air rises is proved on the nineteenth hole . . . regularly.

► On the back of my scorecard, there is a periodic table of the elements.

► I must play golf in
Colorado in the
summertime to see
if altitude really does
have an effect on the
flight of the ball.

I Must Play Golf Today:

ASTROLOGICAL
REASONS

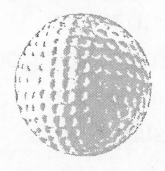

► Little known fact: "Zodiac" actually means "man was born to play golf"— I must honor my destiny.

► My horoscope
suggested that I will
grow rich if I play
golf today with some
unsuspecting suckers.

► Astrology helps me find out who I am and how I can be happier . . . I am golf and golf makes me happy.

► My metaphysical self is manifested on the golf course . . . and on the nineteenth hole.

► I feel whole and complete when Jupiter aligns with Mars.